To my beloved wife Michelle,

Thank you for your continued support and love, and for coming up with idea for the title of the book. I couldn't have done it without you.

To my dear mother and late father,

I dedicate this children's book to both of you as well. If it were not for your foresight, perseverance, and love, my brother and I would not be in the fortunate position we find ourselves in today. Your courage and resolve to make sure we had a better life and the freedom to make our own choices by making the final decision to flee your beloved homeland with literally "nothing in your pockets" is a testament to the dedication you both had to what a family represents. My brother and I owe everything we have to the both of you. I am honored and proud to dedicate this book to you.

Love and respect,

Sam

www.mascotbooks.com

Where Are All My Toys?

©2020 Dr. Sam Rodriguez Morhaim. All Rights Reserved. No part of this publication may be reproduced, stored in a retrieval system or transmitted in any form by any means electronic, mechanical, or photocopying, recording or otherwise without the permission of the author.

For more information, please contact:
Mascot Books
620 Herndon Parkway, Suite 320
Herndon, VA 20170
info@mascotbooks.com

Library of Congress Control Number: 2019905273

CPSIA Code: PRT1119A
ISBN-13: 978-1-64307-571-6

Printed in the United States

Where Are All My Toys?

My Journey from Cuba to America

DR. SAM RODRIGUEZ MORHAIM

illustrated by Walter Policelli

My name is Jimmy Rodriguez and I was born on July 8, 1956, on an island called Cuba. The weather was mostly hot, and there were beaches filled with white sand. Everyone spoke Spanish. I lived here until my family immigrated to the United States, which was just after I turned five years old.

For my fifth birthday, my mom and dad invited all my friends and close family to my party. I got to eat cake, sing birthday songs, and play lots of fun games. Best of all, I got the toy that every kid wanted: Piggy Cook. When you wound him up, he would pretend to cook ham and eggs. It was so cool!

I felt really happy and lucky because I had everything a kid could want. I had family, friends, and, most importantly, lots of new toys!

But the very next day, my mom and dad seemed nervous. They said we were going on a trip as they started packing bags. They told me that I could only bring a few of my favorite toys because we would be coming back soon. I packed crayons and paper, a few toy cars, and of course, Piggy Cook. I still wasn't sure why or exactly where we were going, but I was excited because we were riding on an airplane for the very first time!

When we got to the airport in Cuba, a few policemen stopped us and searched through our suitcases. They began taking things that we weren't allowed to bring on the plane. They took all of my toys and told my mom and dad I couldn't bring *any* of them. Not even Piggy Cook! My dad argued with them, but they didn't seem to care. My mom was so angry because they wouldn't let me take even one toy! I asked my mom, "Where are all my toys?!" She looked at me but didn't say a word. I cried all the way on to the plane and kept yelling, "Where are all my toys?!"

Finally, we arrived on another island in Florida called Miami Beach, where we stayed for several hours while police talked to my dad. We had to go into a building where everyone who left Cuba had to pass something called an "inspection." They took my dad to a room without us to talk to him, and we weren't allowed to see him anymore. A man came out of the room and told my mom that my dad had to stay there, but didn't say why.

My mom asked when we could see my dad again, but they wouldn't tell her. The men who talked to us were immigration officers, and they said we needed to hire someone called a "lawyer" to get him released. For the first time, I could see that my mother was worried about my dad because we didn't have any money to help free him. My mother didn't know what she was going to do without any money. For the first time in my life, I was really scared. I didn't have a house to go to, I didn't have my friends, and worst of all, I didn't have my father. I didn't even care about my toys anymore. I just wanted to see my dad again.

When I asked my mom why we had to leave Cuba, she told me it was complicated. She explained it was because a man named Fidel Castro was going to make kids like me into "little soldiers." When we grew up, they would make us into bigger adult soldiers and force us to carry guns. She said my dad wouldn't let that happen to me, so we had to leave right away. I asked her when we were going to go back to Cuba, but she couldn't tell me. I asked her when we were going to see my dad, but she couldn't tell me. I asked her when I was going to see my friends, but she couldn't tell me.

I remember walking through the streets of Miami for hours, and we were very tired and hungry. We stopped in a store where they sold drinks, but we didn't speak English so it was hard to tell the person in the store what we wanted. Instead, we just pointed to a drink and the man in the store gave it to us—it was called root beer. It was the first time we tried it, and I remember not liking it at all! But we were so thirsty that we drank it anyway.

While we were walking, my mom kept saying that GOD would look out for us. I trusted my mom, so I tried to be strong. As we kept walking, my mom went to make a phone call to a cousin who already lived in America, and to see about finding money for a lawyer to free my dad. My mom walked into a phone booth, and when she looked down, there was a wallet on the ground. When she opened it, it had a lot of money. My mom began to jump up and down, so I started jumping too! My mom told me it was a miracle from God, who left us exactly the right amount of money we needed to get my father a lawyer.

I was happy because my mother was happy, but I was still scared because my dad wasn't with us yet.

After many court hearings during the next month, the lawyer was able to free my dad. He said that my dad was detained because the U.S. government wanted to make sure he didn't support Castro's way of life. The lawyer explained that this kind of thing had happened to other families, too. I remember when my dad first saw us again, he was so happy he didn't even say anything—he just hugged my mom and me. When he did speak, he said, "I will never let anyone take me from you ever again."

The next day, we got on another plane to meet my aunt and uncle in a place called Brooklyn, New York. I was happy to see them, but because there was only one room in their house, we all had to sleep together. It was very crowded. I started to miss my home in Cuba.

We lived with my aunt and uncle for almost a year until my dad got a job and made enough money for us to get our own apartment. My dad was an architect and my mom had been a teacher in Cuba, but she stayed home to take care of me. The apartment we got was even smaller than the one my aunt and uncle had, and it was in a place called New Lots on Sheffield Avenue.

Eventually, it seemed that things were starting to go back to normal, and my mom enrolled me in a new school. I was in the first grade.

Our apartment was so close that I could see my mom through one of the windows in my classroom, and we would wave to each other. I would hold up a picture of something I drew that day. It was really hard at first because I only spoke Spanish and I couldn't understand what anyone was saying! I would sit in a corner all alone and play by myself. None of the other kids would play with me because I didn't speak the same language. They had toys in school, but they weren't like mine. No one had Piggy Cook.

My teacher was really nice and let me draw in class, because my mother told her I liked drawing about my memories of Cuba. The teacher understood how hard it was for me and my family to leave our home in Cuba, so she allowed me to draw during class to help me adjust to all the changes in my life.

I would draw pictures of the beaches in Cuba, my family, my toys, and even my new home in Brooklyn. My teacher thought they were really good, so she hung them up in the classroom. I slowly started to learn how to speak English in school, and I made new friends. I would speak to my family at home in Spanish, and when I got to school, I would only speak English. Eventually, I was so good at speaking English, my teacher appointed me as the "official translator" for all the kids that started arriving from Cuba like myself. I missed my home in Cuba, my friends, and all my toys, but I was quickly getting used to my new life in Brooklyn.

On my sixth birthday, my mom and dad invited my family and my friends from school to celebrate. We did the same things we did on my fifth birthday—my mom decorated the apartment just like she did in Cuba, we ate lots of cake, sang happy birthday, played games, and even had a Mexican piñata filled with candy! But the biggest surprise was yet to come.

The very next morning, my parents woke me up and gave me the most incredible news: they said I was going to be an older brother! I was so excited—even more excited than I was when I got Piggy Cook! I didn't understand where we were going to get him, but my mom explained that he was growing inside her belly and it would take almost a year for him to come.

Everything was changing for the better, but a little part of me still felt unsafe. I was afraid that the police were going to take my toys again. Every night after I played with them, I would hide them under my bed so they wouldn't get taken away. There was also a big box in front of my apartment that had games, balls, and toys that the other kids in the neighborhood played with. I used to take those and hide them, too. I thought I was doing something good, but when my mom found out she was upset.

One day my mom asked me, "Where are all your toys?!" I remember not wanting to tell her because I didn't want to get into trouble for hiding them, but she found them and asked me why they were hidden. I told my mom I was scared that someone would take them. My mom promised me that no one would ever take my toys again, and that now we lived in a country called America that protected us and allowed us to have lots of things—even toys. She also told me that the other toys belonged to the kids in the neighborhood and if I took them, it was considered stealing. She understood why I did it, so I didn't get in trouble, but she made me return them and promise never to take them again.

Over time, I got used to my new apartment and my new toys, and I was getting excited about the arrival of my brother. Most of all, I was grateful to be around my family—we were always together. I felt safe again. I now know that a caring family is the most important thing you can have. I remember thinking that even though my life changed and it was hard at first when we had to leave our country, if you are with people who love you, everything will be okay.

On August 31, 1964, my brother was born—his name was Sam. Mom and Dad brought him home from the hospital, and I got to hold him. He was so small and had really blue eyes like me! I couldn't wait for him to grow up, and I felt happy because no one was going to take *his* toys away. "I won't let anyone take me away from you," I told him. My dad looked at me with a wink, and smiled.

Social Media

Email:
whereareallmytoys@gmail.com

@whereareallmytoys

@whereareallmyt1

@whereareallmytoysbook

About the Author

Sam Rodriguez Morhaim is a Brooklyn native from the small neighborhood of Canarsie. He grew up with both his parents, Julio and Victoria, and one sibling, Jimmy, who is the main character in *Where Are All My Toys?*

His strong sense of family is the result of his parents' determination to provide a normal life for both him and his brother, to the point where they decided to leave their beloved homeland of Cuba in 1962.

As a result of his parents' commitment to education, Sam excelled in school and became a Periodontist. His brother Jaime also became a physician, with a specialty in Dermatology. His desire is not only to achieve professional goals where he is able to help others but personally as well. Sam is the father of three children, Alexander, Daniel, and Isabella. He resides in Oyster Bay, New York, with his wife Michelle. Sam's commitment to fatherhood is what keeps him focused on what's really important in life.

Jimmy and Piggy Cook in Havannah, Cuba in 1962

Mom and Dad at their wedding on July 31, 1955

Mom and Jimmy looking over the harbor in Havannah, Cuba in 1961

Jimmy at home in Cuba in 1962

Jimmy in Parkland, Florida in 2019, decades after his immigration to America

Jimmy's self-portrait of himself as a child, missing his toys

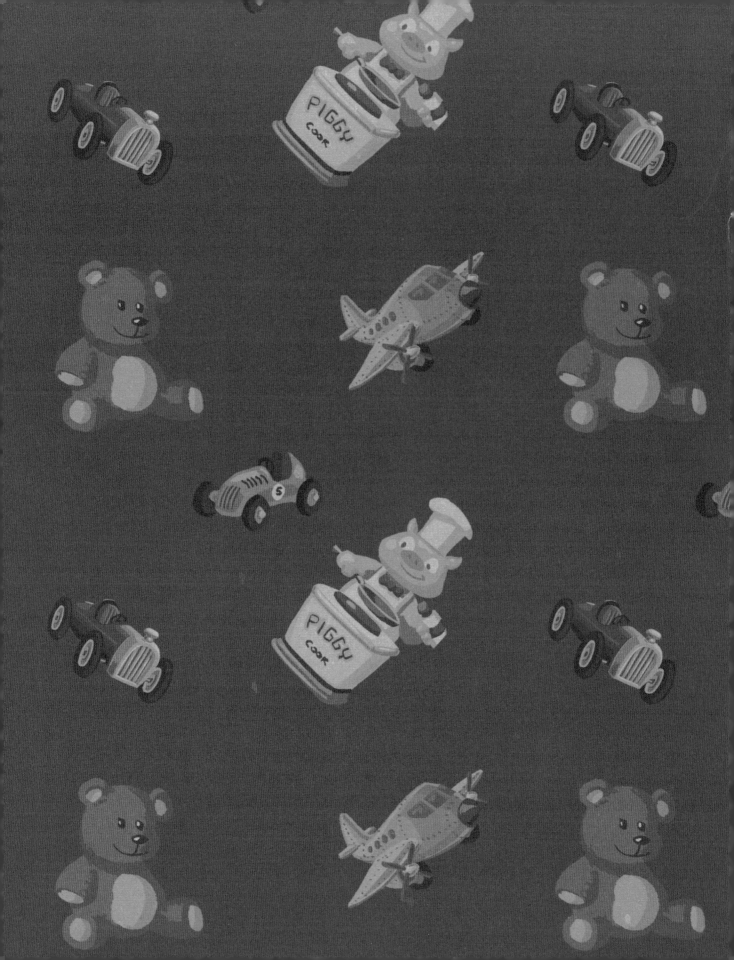